EASY PIANO SOLO

COCKTAIL PIANO CLASSICS

T0039681

ISBN 978-1-4950-5239-2

HAL•LEONARD®
CORPORATION
7777 W. BLUEMOUND RD. P.O. BOX 13819 MILWAUKEE, WI 53213

Visit Hal Leonard Online at
www.halleonard.com

CONTENTS

ALL THE THINGS YOU ARE

from VERY WARM FOR MAY

Lyrics by OSCAR HAMMERSTEIN II
Music by JEROME KERN

Slowly, expressively

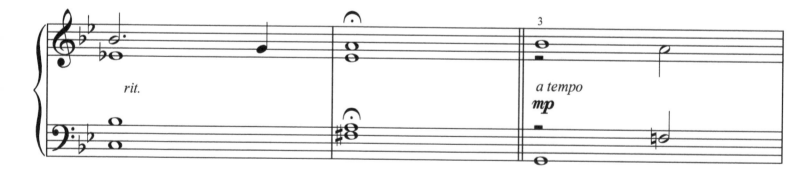

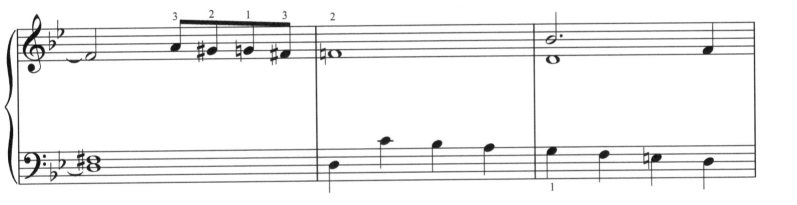

ALWAYS

Words and Music by
IRVING BERLIN

Expressively

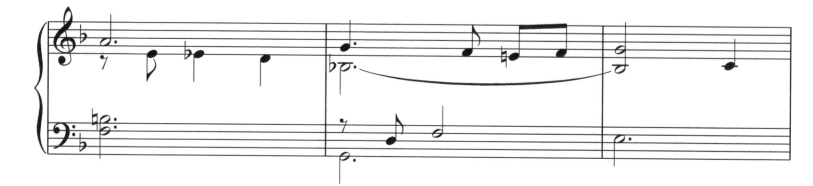

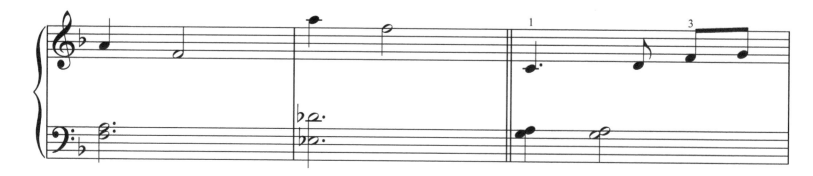

9

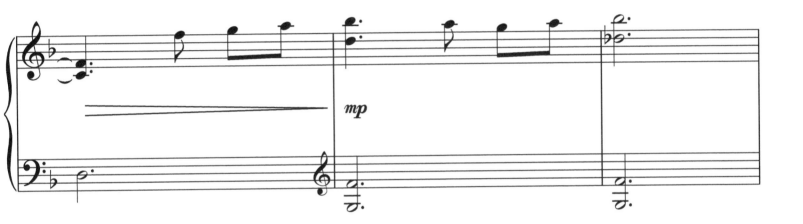

APRIL IN PARIS

Words by E.Y. "YIP" HARBURG
Music by VERNON DUKE

Moderately slow

As Time Goes By

from CASABLANCA

Words and Music by
HERMAN HUPFELD

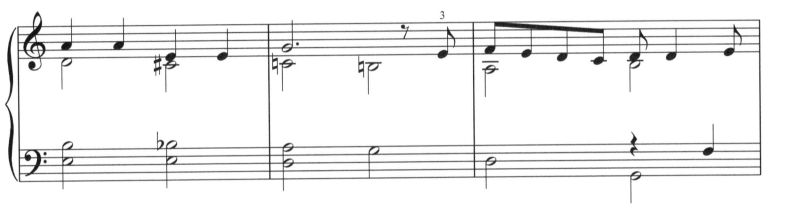

BLUE MOON

Music by RICHARD RODGERS
Lyrics by LORENZ HART

BUT BEAUTIFUL
from ROAD TO RIO

Words by JOHNNY BURKE
Music by JIMMY VAN HEUSEN

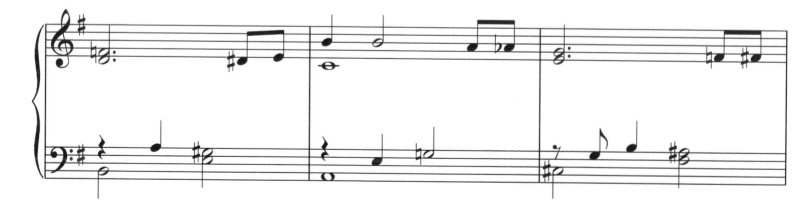

CHEEK TO CHEEK

from the RKO Radio Motion Picture TOP HAT

Words and Music by
IRVING BERLIN

To Coda ⊕

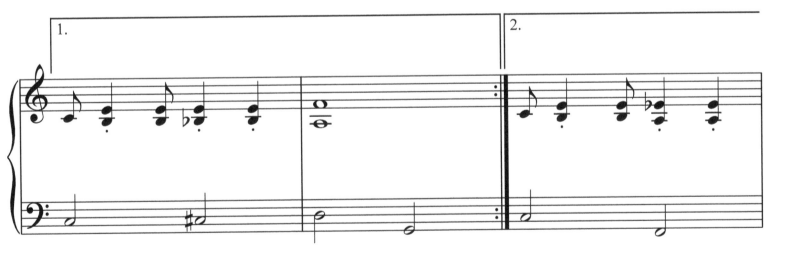

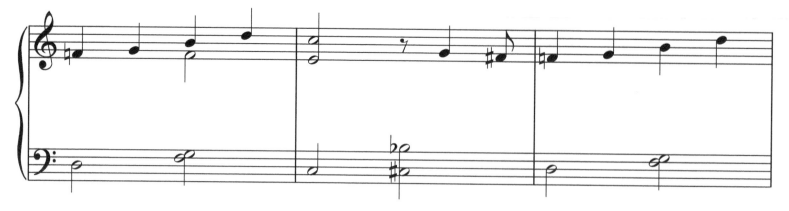

CODA

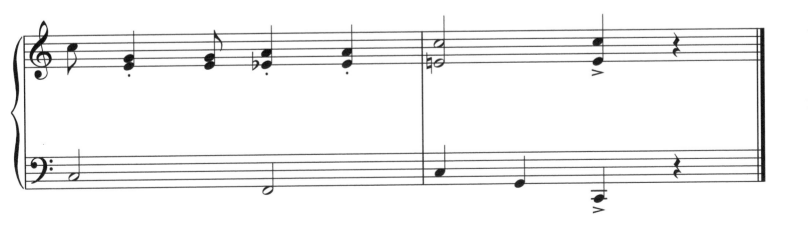

COME RAIN OR COME SHINE

from ST. LOUIS WOMAN

Words by JOHNNY MERCER
Music by HAROLD ARLEN

Moderately slow, bluesy

COCKTAILS FOR TWO

from the Paramount Picture MURDER AT THE VANITIES

Words and Music by ARTHUR JOHNSTON
and SAM COSLOW

DAYS OF WINE AND ROSES

Lyrics by JOHNNY MERCER
Music by HENRY MANCINI

DON'T BLAME ME

Words by DOROTHY FIELDS
Music by JIMMY McHUGH

Moderate Ballad

DREAM A LITTLE DREAM OF ME

Words by GUS KAHN
Music by WILBUR SCHWANDT
and FABIAN ANDREE

Easy Swing

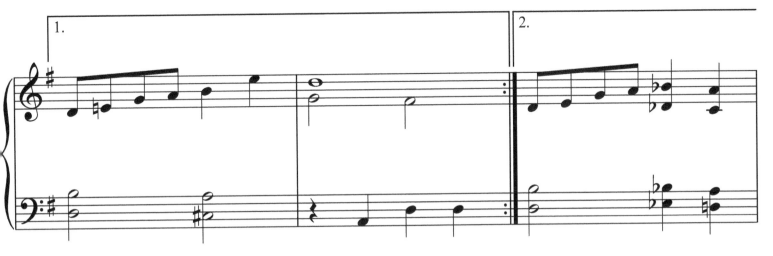

GEORGIA ON MY MIND

Words by STUART GORRELL
Music by HOAGY CARMICHAEL

Slow Ballad

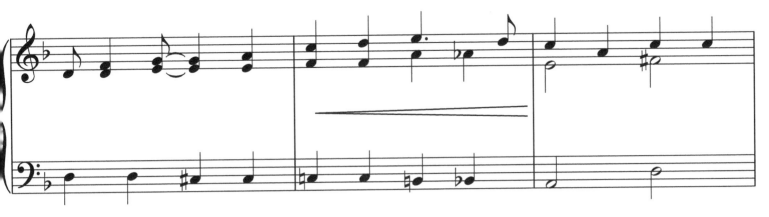

EASY TO LOVE
(You'd Be So Easy to Love)
from BORN TO DANCE

Words and Music by
COLE PORTER

Moderate Bossa Nova

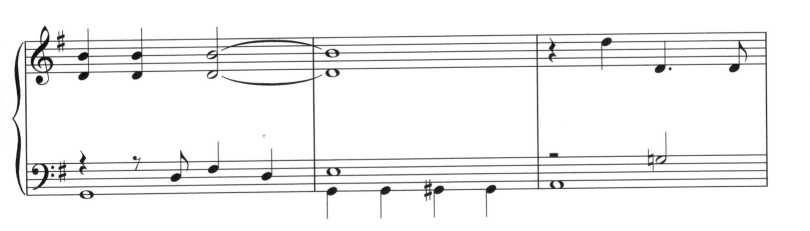

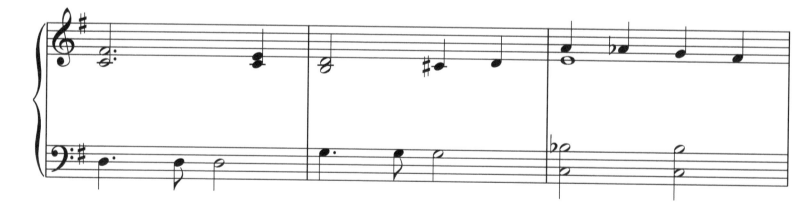

FLY ME TO THE MOON
(In Other Words)

Words and Music by
BART HOWARD

Moderately fast

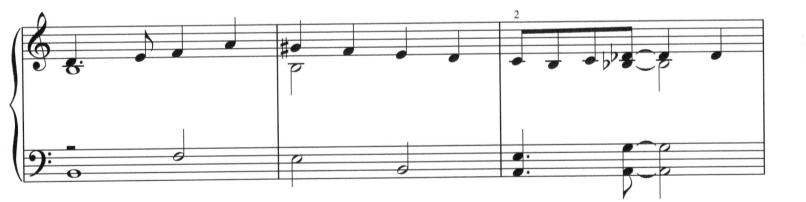

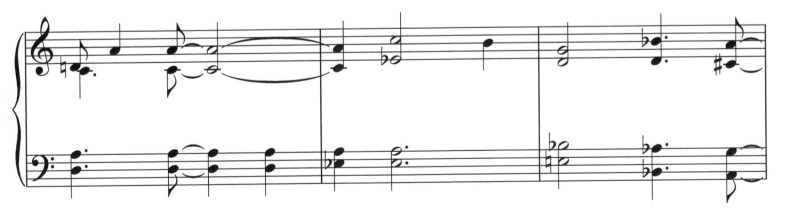

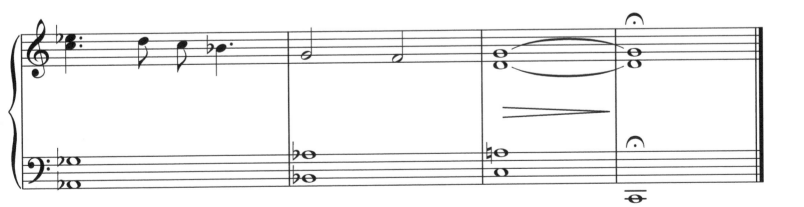

HERE'S THAT RAINY DAY
from CARNIVAL IN FLANDERS

Words by JOHNNY BURKE
Music by JIMMY VAN HEUSEN

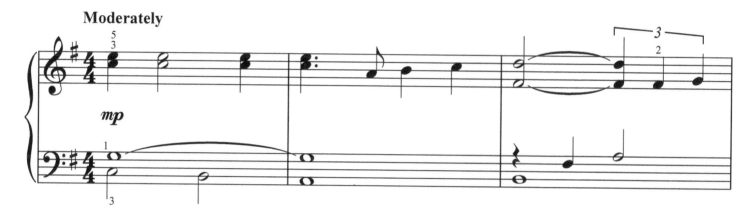

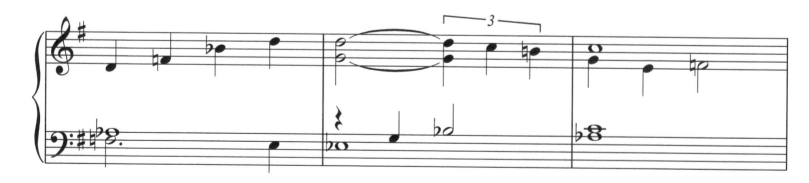

55

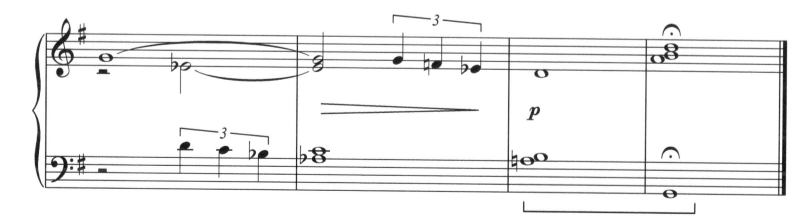

I GOT IT BAD AND THAT AIN'T GOOD

Words by PAUL FRANCIS WEBSTER
Music by DUKE ELLINGTON

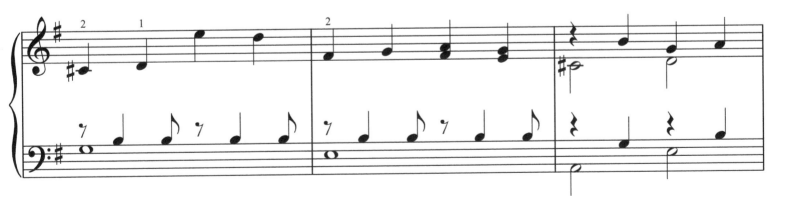

HEY THERE
from THE PAJAMA GAME

Words and Music by RICHARD ADLER
and JERRY ROSS

I LEFT MY HEART IN
SAN FRANCISCO

Words by DOUGLASS CROSS
Music by GEORGE CORY

Freely, with motion

Slower

Moderate Ballad (Swing feel)

poco rall.

mp

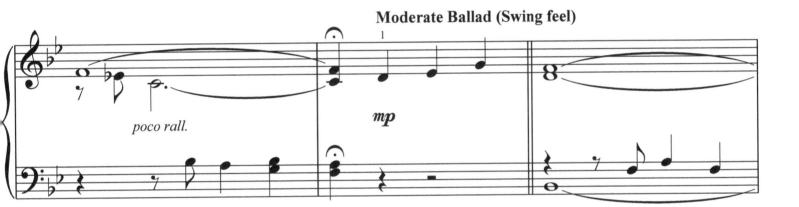

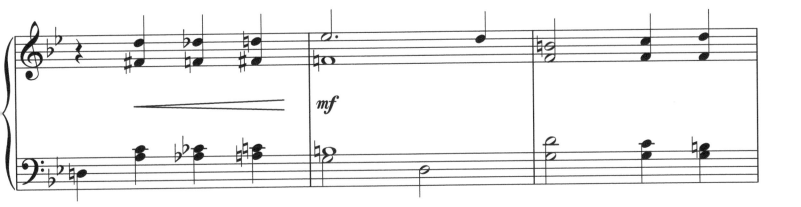

Broadly (♩♩ = ♩♩)

I'LL TAKE ROMANCE

Lyrics by OSCAR HAMMERSTEIN II
Music by BEN OAKLAND

Moderate Waltz

To Coda ⊕

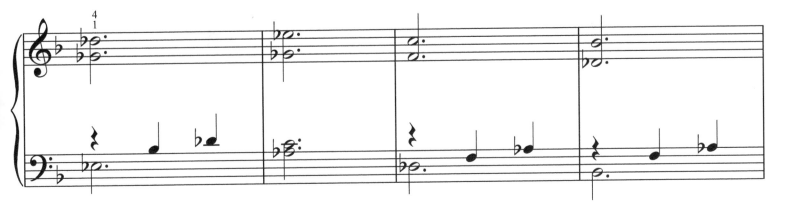

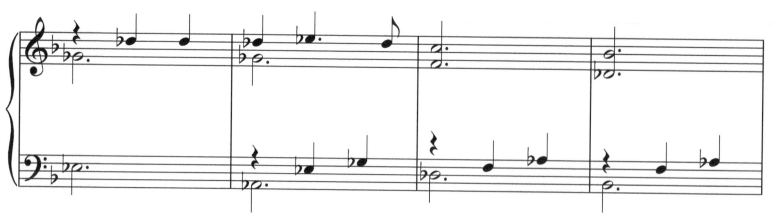

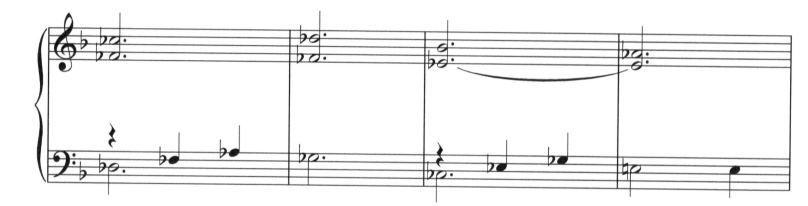

D.S. al Coda

CODA

I'M IN THE MOOD FOR LOVE

Words and Music by JIMMY McHUGH
and DOROTHY FIELDS

I'M OLD FASHIONED

from YOU WERE NEVER LOVELIER

Lyrics by JOHNNY MERCER
Music by JEROME KERN

Moderate, relaxed Swing

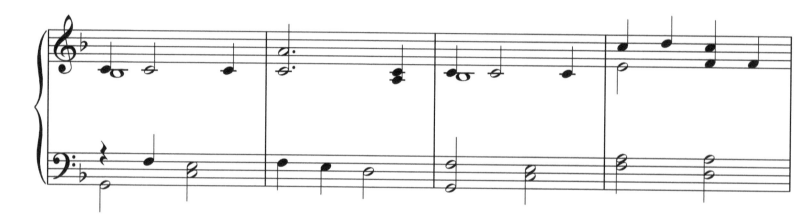

JUST IN TIME

from BELLS ARE RINGING

Words by BETTY COMDEN and ADOLPH GREEN
Music by JULE STYNE

I'VE GOT YOU UNDER MY SKIN

from BORN TO DANCE

Words and Music by
COLE PORTER

Latin Swing feel

THE LADY IS A TRAMP

from BABES IN ARMS

Words by LORENZ HART
Music by RICHARD RODGERS

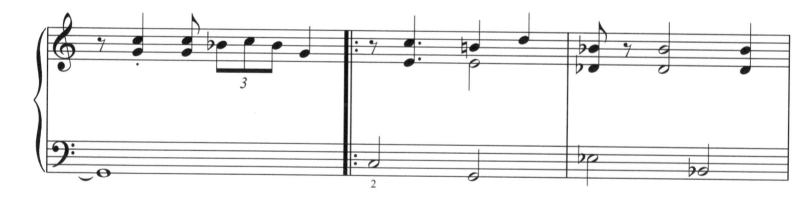

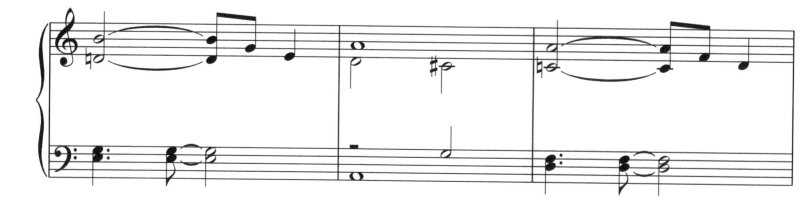

LAURA

Lyrics by JOHNNY MERCER
Music by DAVID RAKSIN

Freely

Moderate Ballad, flowing

LONG AGO
(And Far Away)
from COVER GIRL

Music by IRA GERSHWIN
Music by JEROME KERN

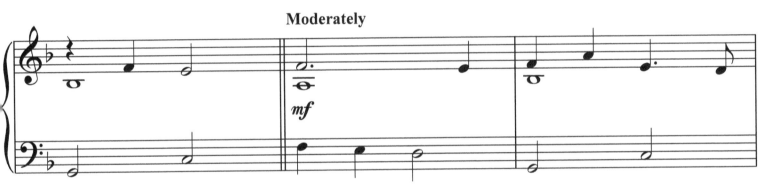

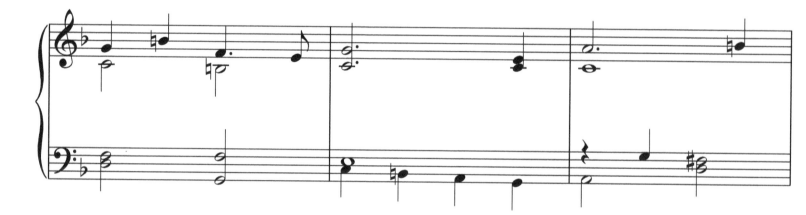

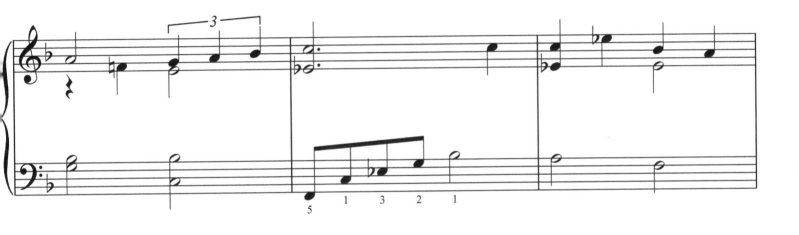

Freely

MACK THE KNIFE
from THE THREEPENNY OPERA

English Words by MARC BLITZSTEIN
Original German Words by BERT BRECHT
Music by KURT WEILL

Moderate Swing

LULLABY OF BIRDLAND

Words by GEORGE DAVID WEISS
Music by GEORGE SHEARING

Moderate Swing

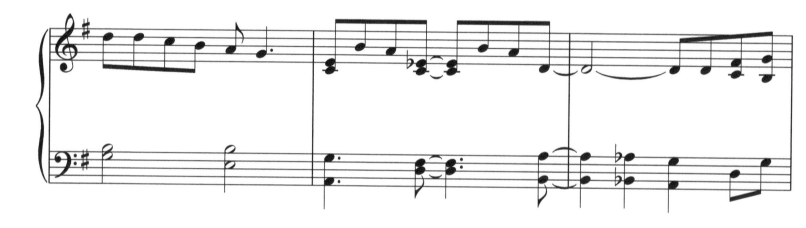

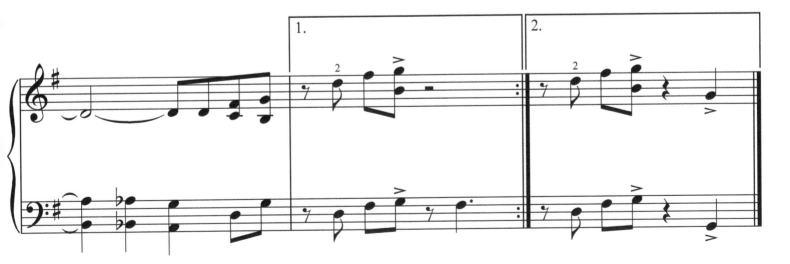

MOONLIGHT BECOMES YOU
from the Paramount Picture ROAD TO MOROCCO

Words by JOHNNY BURKE
Music by JAMES VAN HEUSEN

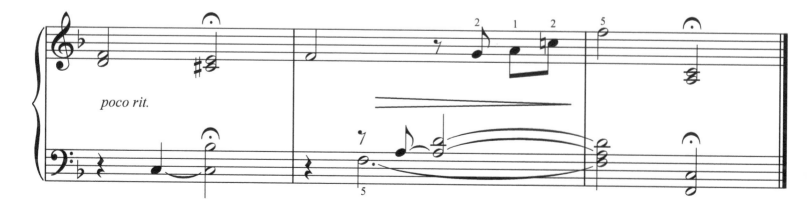

poco rit.

MOON RIVER
from the Paramount Picture BREAKFAST AT TIFFANY'S

Words by JOHNNY MERCER
Music by HENRY MANCINI

Moderately slow

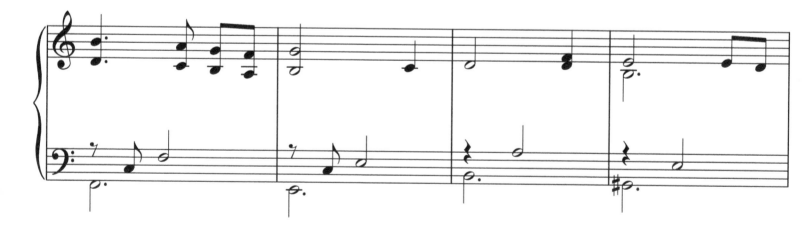

Slower

MORE
(Ti guarderò nel cuore)
from the film MONDO CANE

Music by NINO OLIVIERO and RIZ ORTOLANI
Italian Lyrics by MARCELLO CIORCIOLINI
English Lyrics by NORMAN NEWELL

Bossa Nova

poco rit.

MORE THAN YOU KNOW

Words by WILLIAM ROSE and EDWARD ELISCU
Music by VINCENT YOUMANS

Moderately slow

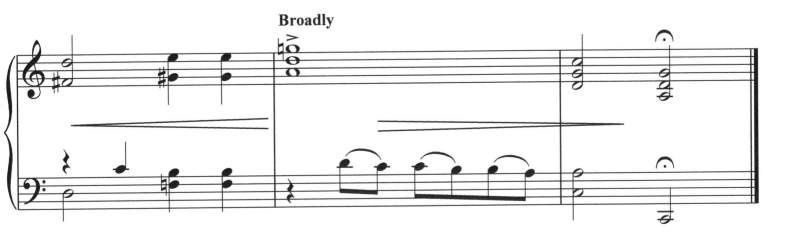

A NIGHTINGALE SANG IN BERKELEY SQUARE

Lyric by ERIC MASCHWITZ
Music by MANNING SHERWIN

Slowly

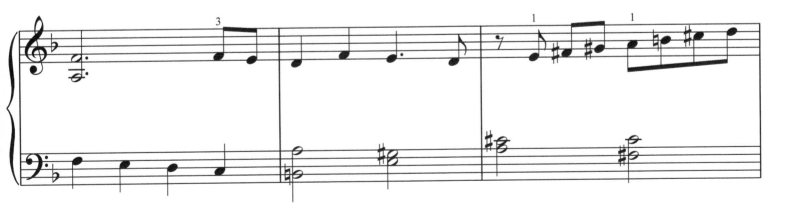

Freely

poco rit.

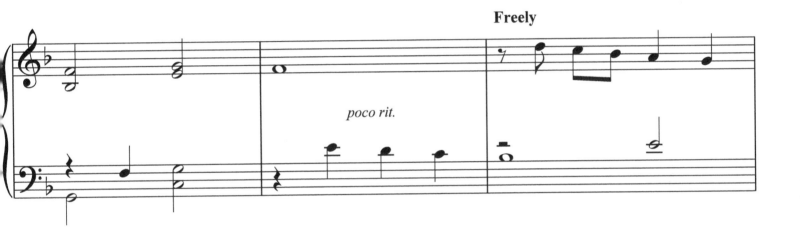

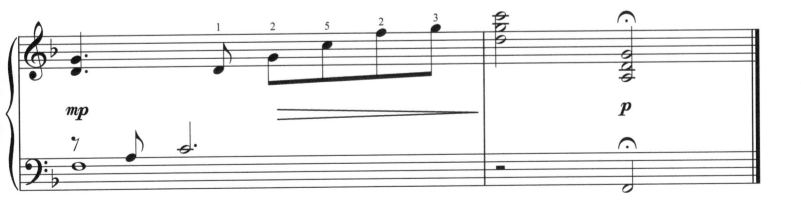

mp

p

ONCE IN A WHILE

Words by BUD GREEN
Music by MICHAEL EDWARDS

Moderately

OUT OF NOWHERE

from the Paramount Picture DUDE RANCH

Words by EDWARD HEYMAN
Music by JOHNNY GREEN

Moderate Swing

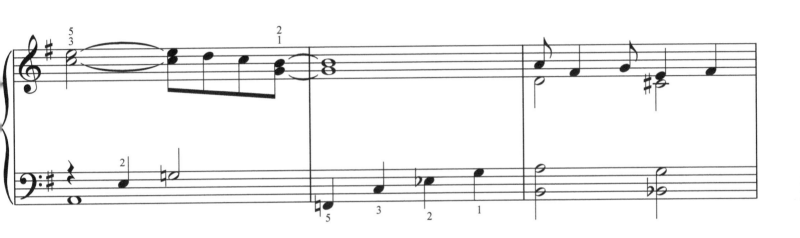

OVER THE RAINBOW
from THE WIZARD OF OZ

Music by HAROLD ARLEN
Lyric by E.Y. "YIP" HARBURG

Freely, with expression

Moderately slow

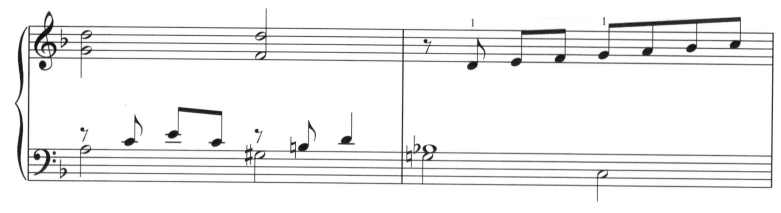

a little slower, freely

PEOPLE
from FUNNY GIRL

Words by BOB MERRILL
Music by JULE STYNE

a little slower

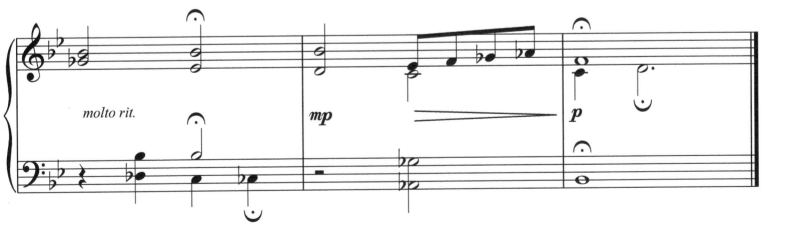

molto rit.

mp

p

PUTTIN' ON THE RITZ

Words and Music by
IRVING BERLIN

SEPTEMBER IN THE RAIN

Words by AL DUBIN
Music by HARRY WARREN

Moderate Bossa Nova

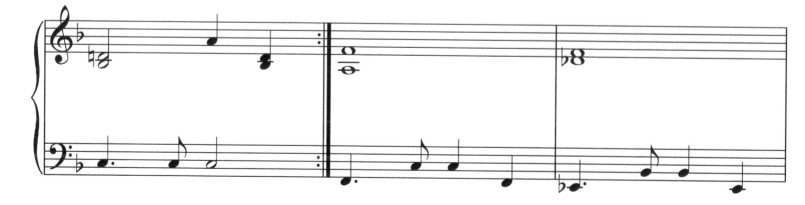

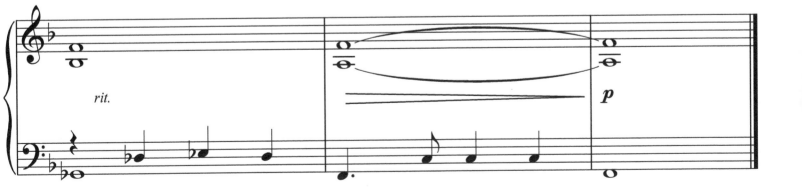

SPEAK LOW
from the Musical Production ONE TOUCH OF VENUS

Words by OGDEN NASH
Music by KURT WEILL

Moderate Latin feel

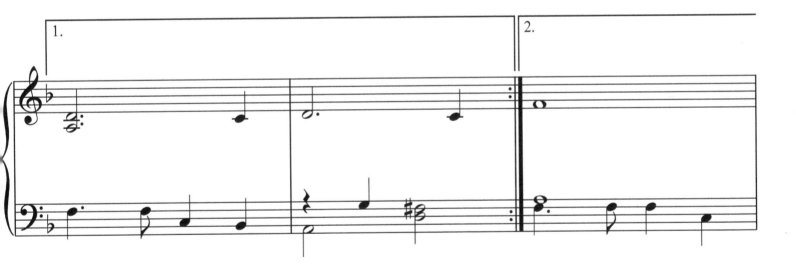

STARDUST

Music by HOAGY CARMICHAEL

Moderately, rubato

Steady Ballad tempo

a little slower

(Theme from)
A SUMMER PLACE
from A SUMMER PLACE

Words by MACK DISCANT
Music by MAX STEINER

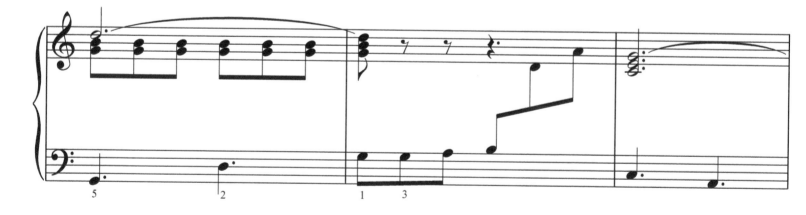

rit.

TENDERLY
from TORCH SONG

Lyric by JACK LAWRENCE
Music by WALTER GROSS

Easy, relaxed Waltz

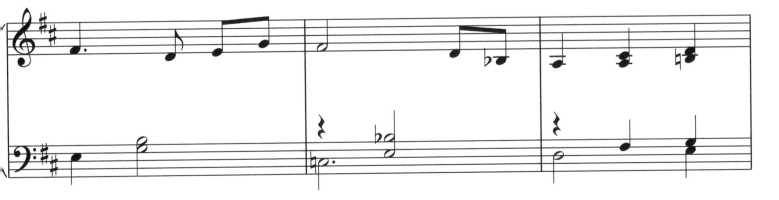

To Coda

D.S. al Coda

CODA

A little slower

rit.

mp

Freely

rit.

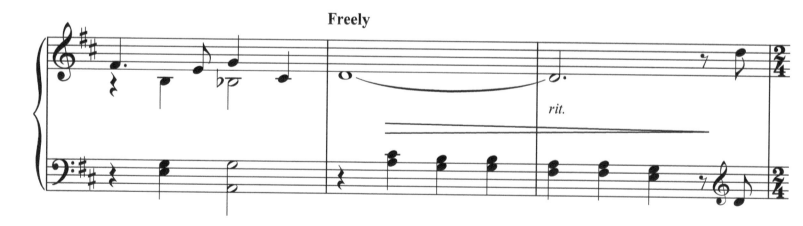

Slowly

THERE WILL NEVER BE ANOTHER YOU

from the Motion Picture ICELAND

Lyric by MACK GORDON
Music by HARRY WARREN

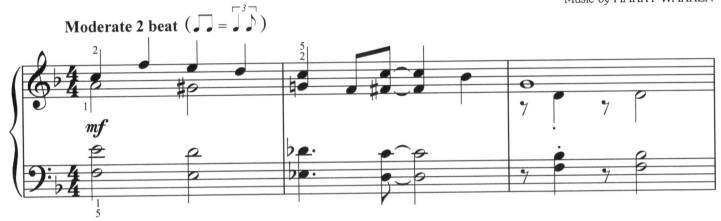

THE VERY THOUGHT OF YOU

Words and Music by
RAY NOBLE

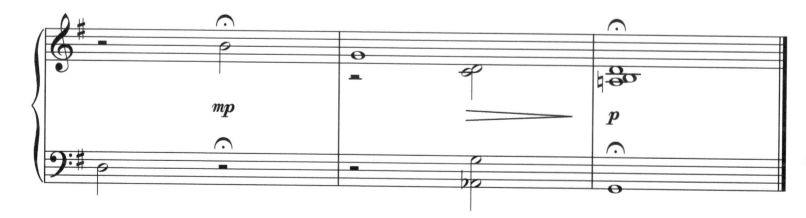

The Way You Look Tonight

from SWING TIME

Words by DOROTHY FIELDS
Music by JEROME KERN

Moderate Swing

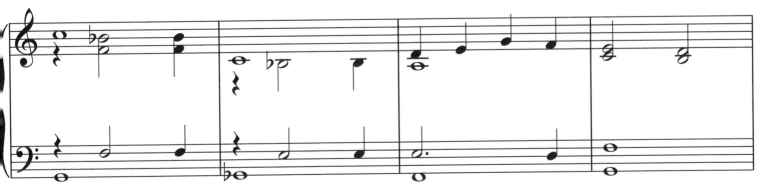

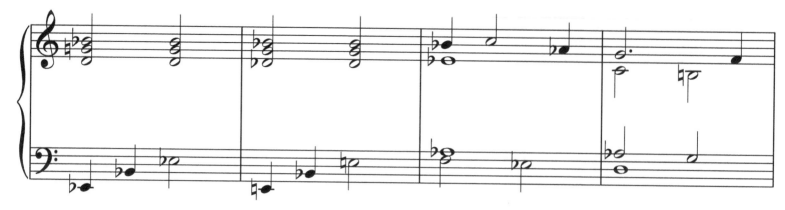

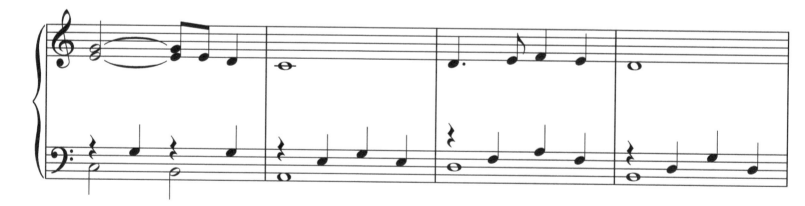

WHEN SUNNY GETS BLUE

Lyric by JACK SEGAL
Music by MARVIN FISHER

YESTERDAYS
from ROBERTA

Words by OTTO HARBACH
Music by JEROME KERN

Moderate Bossa Nova

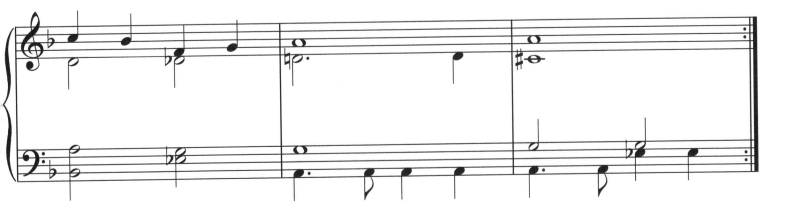

YOUNG AND FOOLISH

from PLAIN AND FANCY

Words by ARNOLD B. HORWITT
Music by ALBERT HAGUE

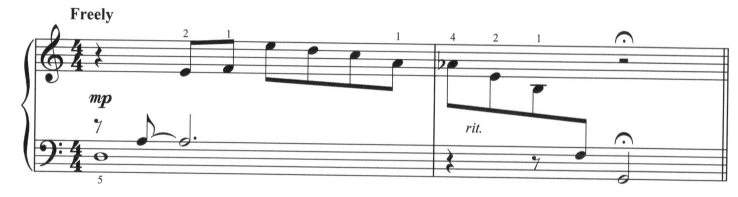

cresc.

mp

A little slower

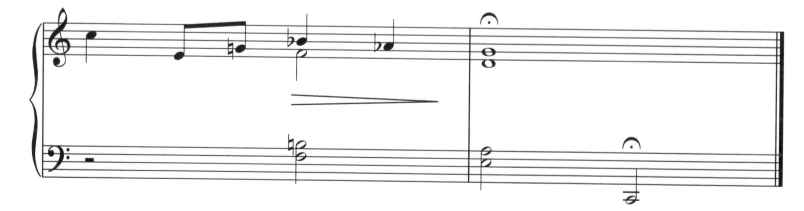